Y0-BRF-792

To:

Phyllis Moore

From:

New Palestine Baptist Church

Date:

5-11-2003 Mother's Day

smiles
Mom *for*

When We Smile at God,
He Smiles Back

smiles

for Mom

Brighton Books
Nashville, TN 37203

ISBN 1-58334-203-6

The quoted ideas expressed in this book (but not scripture verses) are not, in all cases, exact quotations, as some have been edited for clarity and brevity. In all cases, the author has attempted to maintain the speaker's original intent. In some cases, quoted material for this book was obtained from secondary sources, primarily print media. While every effort was made to ensure the accuracy of these sources, the accuracy cannot be guaranteed. For additions, deletions, corrections or clarifications in future editions of this text, please write Brighton Books.

Printed in the United States of America
Cover Design & Page Layout: Bart Dawson

1 2 3 4 5 6 7 8 9 10 • 03 04 05 06 07 08 09 10

To Great Moms
Who Love to Smile

Table of Contents

Introduction

Who deserves a smile more than Mom? Nobody!

Mothers give life and they teach life. They care for us when we're sick, and they love us when we deserve it—and when we don't. Our mothers never stop caring or sharing, and they have earned all the good and beautiful things that this world holds, including our smiles. But, our mothers also deserve a peace that is beyond the limitations of this earth. That peace is God's peace.

This book is intended to make mothers smile. But it is also intended to remind readers that God, through His Son, Jesus, is the ultimate source of joy and salvation. We are able to smile—today and throughout eternity—because God first smiled upon us. And now, it's our turn to share God's smile with a world that desperately needs His healing grace and His miraculous love.

Smiles for Mom

A happy heart makes
the face cheerful.
Proverbs 15:13 NIV

Those who are God's
without reserve are,
in every sense, content.

Hannah Whitall Smith

Okay, Mom, it's been a typical day. You've cared for your family, worked your fingers to the bone, rushed from point A to point Z, and taken barely a moment for yourself. But have you taken time to smile? If so, you're a very wise woman. If not, it's time to slow down, to take a deep breath, and to recount your blessings!

God has promised all of us *the opportunity* to experience spiritual abundance and peace. But, it's up to *each of us* to claim the spiritual riches that God has in store. God promises us a life of fulfillment and joy, but He does not force His joy upon us.

Would you like to experience the peace and the joy that God intends for you? Then accept His Son and lay claim to His promises. And then, put a smile on your face that stretches all the way down to your heart. When you do, you'll discover that when you smile at God, He smiles back.

Rejoice, and be exceeding glad:
for great is your reward in heaven . . . .
Matthew 5:12 KJV

When the dream of our heart is one
that God has planted there, a strange
happiness flows into us. At that moment,
all of the spiritual resources of the universe
are released to help us. Our praying is then
at one with the will of God and becomes
a channel for the Creator's purposes
for us and our world.

Catherine Marshall

One of the great joys of the great Father's
heart is to make His children glad.

C. H. Spurgeon

Make God's will the focus of your life
day by day. If you seek to please Him
and Him alone, you'll find yourself
satisfied with life.

Kay Arthur

Delight thyself also in
the LORD; and he shall give
thee the desires of thine heart.

Psalm 37:4 KJV

We must meet our disappointments,
our persecutions, our malicious enemies,
our provoking friends, our trials and
temptations of every sort, with an attitude
of surrender and trust. We must spread
our wings and "mount up" to the "heavenly
places in Christ" above them all, where
they will lose their power to harm
or distress us.

Hannah Whitall Smith

Happiness is the byproduct of a life that
is lived in the will of God. When we
humbly serve others, walk in God's path
of holiness, and do what He tells us,
then we will enjoy happiness.

Warren Wiersbe

Holy activity is the mother of holy joy.

C. H. Spurgeon

Joy has nothing to do with circumstances.
Joy is a choice. It is a matter of attitude
that stems from one's confidence in God.

Charles Swindoll

Christ is not only a remedy for your
weariness and trouble, but He will give
you an abundance of the contrary: joy and
delight. They who come to Christ do not
only come to a resting-place after they
have been wandering in a wilderness, but
they come to a banqueting-house where
they may rest, and where they may feast.
They may cease from their former troubles
and toils, and they may enter upon
a course of delights and spiritual joys.

Jonathan Edwards

Joy comes not
from what we have
but from what we are.

C. H. Spurgeon

Then spake Jesus again
unto them, saying,
I am the light of the world:
he that followeth me
shall not walk in darkness,
but shall have the light of life.

John 8:12 KJV

This is the day which
the Lord hath made; we will
rejoice and be glad in it.

Psalm 118:24 KJV

God's Love

For God so loved the world
that he gave his one and only
Son, that whoever believes
in him shall not perish but
have eternal life.
John 3:16 NIV

The essence of God's being is love—He never separates Himself from that.

Kay Arthur

*B*eing a mother, you know the profound love that you hold in your heart for your own children. As a child of God, you can only imagine the infinite love that your Heavenly Father holds for you.

God made you in His own image and gave you salvation through the person of His Son, Jesus Christ. And now, precisely because you are a wondrous creation treasured by God, a question presents itself: What will you do in response to the Creator's love? Will you ignore it or embrace it? Will you return it or neglect it? That decision, of course, is yours and yours alone.

When you embrace God's love, you are forever changed. When you embrace God's love, you feel differently about yourself, your neighbors, your family, and your world. More importantly, you share God's message—and His love—with others.

The Heavenly Father—a God of infinite love and mercy—is waiting to embrace you with open arms. Accept His love today and forever.

The Lord is full of compassion and mercy.
James 5:11 NIV

Accepting God's love as a gift instead of
trying to earn it had somehow seemed
presumptuous and arrogant to me, when,
in fact, my pride was tricking me into
thinking that I could merit His love and
forgiveness with my own strength.

Lisa Whelchel

God loves us the way we are,
but He loves us too much
to leave us that way.

Leighton Ford

It was not the soldiers who killed Him,
nor the screams of the mob:
It was His devotion to us.

Max Lucado

The love of God is revealed in that He
laid down His life for His enemies.

Oswald Chambers

"How can I give you up, Ephraim?
How can I hand you over, Israel?"
Substitute your own name for Ephraim
and Israel. At the heart of the gospel is
a God who deliberately surrenders to
the wild, irresistible power of love.

Philip Yancey

Jesus loves us with fidelity, purity,
constancy, and passion, no matter how
imperfect we are.

Stormie Omartian

Even when we cannot see the why and
wherefore of God's dealings, we know
that there is love in and behind them,
so we can rejoice always.

J. I. Packer

God's mercy is infinite, but it always flows
to men through the golden channel
of Jesus Christ, His Son.

C. H. Spurgeon

God is more anxious to
bestow His blessings on us
than we are to receive them.

St. Augustine

There is no pit so deep that God's love
is not deeper still.

Corrie ten Boom

God's promises are overflowings
from His great heart.

C. H. Spurgeon

Therefore humble yourselves under
the mighty hand of God, that He may
exalt you at the proper time,
casting all your anxiety on Him,
because He cares for you.

1 Peter 5:6-7 NASB

O praise the LORD,
all ye nations: praise him,
all ye people. For his merciful
kindness is great toward us:
and the truth of the LORD
endureth for ever.
Praise ye the LORD.

Psalm 117:1-2 KJV

You are my God, and I will
give you thanks; you are
my God, and I will exalt you.
Give thanks to the LORD,
for he is good; his love
endures forever.

Psalm 118:28-29 NIV

Laughter

A cheerful heart is good
medicine, but a broken spirit
saps a person's strength.
Proverbs 17:22 NLT

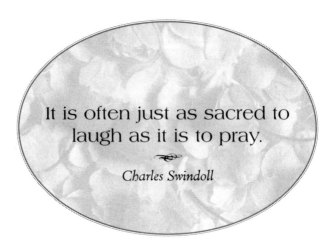

It is often just as sacred to
laugh as it is to pray.

Charles Swindoll

Motherhood is no laughing matter; it should be taken very seriously, up to a point. But no mother's responsibilities should be so burdensome that she forgets to laugh. Laughter is medicine for the soul, but sometimes, amid the stresses of the day, we forget to take our medicine. Instead of viewing our world with a mixture of optimism and humor, we allow worries and distractions to rob us of the joy that God intends for our lives.

If your heart is heavy, open the door of your soul to Christ. He will give you peace and joy. And, if you already have the joy of Christ in your heart, share it freely, just as Christ freely shared His joy with you. As you go about your daily activities, approach life with a smile on your lips and hope in your heart. And laugh every chance you get. After all, God created laughter for a reason . . . and Father indeed knows best. So laugh!

A happy heart makes the face cheerful . . . .
Proverbs 15:13 NIV

A keen sense of humor helps
us to overlook the unbecoming,
understand the unconventional,
tolerate the unpleasant,
overcome the unexpected,
and outlast the unbearable.

Billy Graham

There is a time for everything,
and a season for every activity
under heaven . . . a time to
weep and a time to laugh,
a time to mourn and
a time to dance . . . .

Ecclesiastes 3:1,4 NIV

If you're not allowed to laugh in heaven,
I don't want to go there.

Martin Luther

Do not let your happiness depend on
something you may lose, but only upon
the Beloved who will never pass away.

C. S. Lewis

Happiness is obedience, and
         obedience is happiness.

C. H. Spurgeon

He who pursues righteousness and
    love finds life, prosperity and honor.

Proverbs 21:21 NIV

Be cheerful no matter what; pray all
    the time; thank God no matter what
happens. This is the way God wants you
    who belong to Christ Jesus to live.

1 Thessalonians 5:16-18 MSG

If our hearts have been attuned
to God through an abiding faith
in Christ, the result will be
joyous optimism and
good cheer.

Billy Graham

A child of God should be
a visible beatitude for
happiness and a living
doxology for gratitude.

❧

C. H. Spurgeon

Shout for joy to the LORD,
all the earth, burst into jubilant
song with music; make music
to the LORD with the harp,
with the harp and the sound
of singing, with trumpets and
the blast of the ram's horn—
shout for joy before
the LORD, the King.

Psalm 98:4-6 NIV

Joy

May the God of hope fill you with all joy and peace as you trust in him, so that you may overflow with hope by the power of the Holy Spirit.

Romans 15:13 NIV

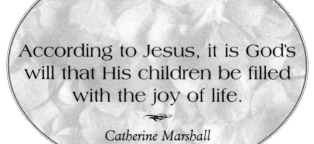

According to Jesus, it is God's
will that His children be filled
with the joy of life.

Catherine Marshall

*J*oni Eareckson Tada spoke for Christian women of every generation when she observed, "I wanted the deepest part of me to vibrate with that ancient yet familiar longing—that desire for something that would fill and overflow my soul."

God's plan for our lives includes great joy, but our Heavenly Father will not force His joy upon us. We must accept God's peace by genuinely welcoming His Son into our hearts.

Let us praise the Creator for His priceless gift, and let us share His Good News with the world. Let us share the Father's promises, His love, and His joy. When we do, we are eternally blessed, and so are our families, our friends, and all whom God has chosen to place along our paths.

And let the peace of the Messiah,
to which you were also called in one body,
control your hearts. Be thankful.
Colossians 3:15 HCSB

The happiest people in the world are
   not those who have no problems, but
the people who have learned to live with
   those things that are less than perfect.
James Dobson

In commanding us to glorify Him,
   God is inviting us to enjoy Him.
C. S. Lewis

Thou wilt show me the path
of life: in thy presence *is*
fulness of joy; at thy right
hand *there are* pleasures
for evermore.

Psalm 16:11 KJV

Our obedience does not make God
any bigger or better than He already is.
Anything God commands of us is so that
our joy may be full—the joy of seeing His
glory revealed to us and in us!

Beth Moore

When Jesus Christ is the source of our joy,
no words can describe it.

Billy Graham

The LORD is king!
Let the earth rejoice!
Let the farthest islands be glad.

Psalm 97:1 NLT

There seems to be a chilling fear of holy
enthusiasm among the people of God.
We try to tell how happy we are—but
we remain so well-controlled that there
are very few waves of glory experienced
in our midst.

A. W. Tozer

God knows everything. He can manage
everything, and He loves us. Surely this
is enough for a fullness of joy
that is beyond words.

Hannah Whitall Smith

Each day, each moment is
so pregnant with eternity that
if we "tune in" to it, we can
hardly contain the joy.

Gloria Gaither

In the absence of all other joys,
the joy of the Lord can fill
the soul to the brim.

C. H. Spurgeon

The Bible instructs—and experience
   teaches—that praising God results
in our burdens being lifted and our joys
   being multiplied.

Jim Gallery

What is your focus today? Joy comes
   when it is Jesus first, others second . . .
         then you.

Kay Arthur

Oh, the tranquil joy of that dear retreat,
   Where the Savior bids thee rest,
With steadfast hope, and a trusting faith,
   In His love secure and blest.

Fanny Crosby

For the LORD your God has
arrived to live among you.
He is a mighty savior. He will
rejoice over you with great
gladness. With his love,
he will calm all your fears.
He will exult over you by
singing a happy song.

❧

Zephaniah 3:17 NLT

Peace

The peace of God, which
passeth all understanding,
shall keep your hearts and
minds through Christ Jesus.

Philippians 4:7 KJV

If you want to hear God's voice clearly and you are uncertain, then remain in His presence until He changes that uncertainty. Often much can happen during this waiting for the Lord. Sometimes He changes pride into humility; doubt into faith and peace . . . .

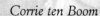

Corrie ten Boom

For busy mothers, a moment's peace can be a scarce commodity. But no matter how numerous the interruptions and demands of the day, God is ever-present, always ready and willing to offer solace to those who seek "the peace that passes all understanding."

Have you found the genuine peace that can be yours through Jesus Christ? Or are you still rushing after the illusion of "peace and happiness" that the world promises but cannot deliver? Today, as a gift to yourself, to your family, and to your friends, claim the inner peace that is your spiritual birthright: the peace of Jesus Christ. It is offered freely; it has been paid for in full; it is yours for the asking. So ask. And then share.

Those who love Your law have great peace,
and nothing causes them to stumble.
Psalm 119:165 NASB

Rejoicing is a matter of obedience
    to God—an obedience that will start you
    on the road to peace and contentment.
                                    Kay Arthur

Jesus gives us the ultimate rest,
        the confidence we need, to escape
            the frustration and chaos of
                the world around us.
                                    Billy Graham

The more closely you cling to
the Lord Jesus, the more clear
will your peace be.

C. H. Spurgeon

The ideal of man is to live in peace
and die in serenity.

St. Augustine

"My peace I give unto you"; it is a peace
all over from the crown of the head
to the sole of the feet,
an irrepressible confidence.

Oswald Chambers

Jesus said, "Blessed are the peacemakers:
for they shall be called the children of
God." Where does peacemaking begin?
There can be no peace until
we find peace with God.

Billy Graham

Come to me, all you who are weary and burdened, and I will give you rest. Take my yoke upon you and learn from me, for I am gentle and humble in heart, and you will find rest for your souls. For my yoke is easy and my burden is light.

Matthew 11:28-30 NIV

And let the peace of God rule
in your hearts . . .
and be ye thankful.

Colossians 3:15 KJV

And the work of righteousness will be
peace, And the service of righteousness,
quietness and confidence forever.

Isaiah 32:17 NASB

To know God as He really is—in His
essential nature and character—is to arrive
at a citadel of peace that circumstances
may storm, but can never capture.

Catherine Marshall

Now God designed the human machine
to run on Himself. God cannot give
us happiness and peace apart from
Himself, because it is not there.
There is no such thing.

C. S. Lewis

And the peace of God, which surpasses every thought, will guard your hearts and your minds in Christ Jesus. Finally brothers, whatever is true, whatever is honorable, whatever is just, whatever is pure, whatever is lovely, whatever is commendable— if there is any moral excellence and if there is any praise— dwell on these things.

Philippians 4:7-8 HCSB

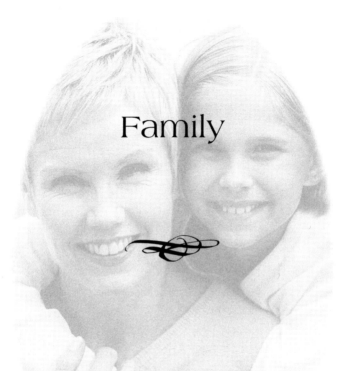

Family

Choose for yourselves this day
whom you will serve . . .
as for me and my household,
we will serve the LORD.

Joshua 24:15 NIV

A home is a place where
we find direction.

Gigi Graham Tchividjian

*A*s every mother knows, family life is a mixture of conversations, mediations, irritations, deliberations, commiserations, frustrations, negotiations, and celebrations. In other words, the life of the typical mom is incredibly varied.

Certainly, in the life of every family, there are moments of frustration and disappointment. Lots of them. But, for those who are blessed to live in the presence of a close-knit, caring clan, the rewards far outweigh the frustrations.

No family is perfect; and, despite the inevitable challenges and occasional hurt feelings of family life, your clan is God's gift to you. That little band of men, women, kids, and babies is a priceless treasure on temporary loan from the Father above. Give thanks to the Giver for the gift of family . . . and act accordingly.

Unless the LORD builds a house, the work of the builders is useless.
Psalm 127:1 NLT

We must strengthen our commitment
to model strong families ourselves, to live
by godly priorities in a culture where self
so often supersedes commitment to others.
And, as we not only model but assertively
reach out to help others, we must realize
that even huge societal problems are
solved one person at a time.

Chuck Colson

It is a reverent thing to see an ancient
castle or building not in decay, or to see
a fair timber tree sound and perfect. How
much more beautiful it is to behold an
ancient and noble family that has stood
against the waves and weathers of time.

Francis Bacon

The secret of a happy home life is that
the members of the family learn
to give and receive love.

Billy Graham

The only true source of meaning in life
is found in love for God and His son
Jesus Christ, and love for mankind,
beginning with our own families.

James Dobson

No other structure can replace the family.
Without it, our children have no moral
foundation. Without it, they become moral
illiterates whose only law is self.

Chuck Colson

The Golden Rule begins
at home.

Marie T. Freeman

Family

We should live so that everybody knows
we're Christians, and most of all,
our families ought to know.
D. L. Moody

Never give your family the leftovers
and crumbs of your time.
Charles Swindoll

You have heard about "quality time"
and "quantity time."
Your family needs both.
Jim Gallery

Apart from religious influence,
the family is the most important
influence on society.

Billy Graham

A family is a place where principles
are hammered and honed on
the anvil of everyday living.

Charles Swindoll

Brotherly love is still the distinguishing
badge of every true Christian.

Matthew Henry

These should learn first of all to put their
religion into practice by caring
for their own family.

1 Timothy 5:4 NIV

He blesses the home
of the righteous.

Proverbs 3:33 NIV

Hope

You are my hope; O Lord GOD,
You are my confidence.
Psalm 71:5 NASB

Our hope in Christ for the future is
the mainstream of our joy.
C. H. Spurgeon

This hope we have as an anchor of
the soul, a hope both sure and steadfast.
Hebrews 6:19 NASB

*A*re you a hope-filled mom? You should be. After all, God is good; His love endures; and He has offered you the priceless gift of eternal life. And, God has blessed you with a loving family. But, in the darker moments of life, it's easy to lose hope.

When a suffering woman sought healing by merely touching the hem of His cloak, Jesus replied, "Daughter, be of good comfort; thy faith hath made thee whole" (Matthew 9:24 KJV). The message to believers is clear: if we are to be made whole by God, we must live by faith. But, when we face adversity, anxiety, or heartbreak, living by faith can be difficult indeed. Still, God remains faithful to us, and we should remain faithful to Him.

If you find yourself falling into the traps of worry and discouragement, seek the healing touch of Jesus and the encouraging words of fellow Christians. This world can be a place of trials and tribulations, but as believers, we are secure. God has promised us peace, joy, and eternal life. And, of course, God keeps His promises today, tomorrow, and forever.

Hope is no other than the expectation
of those things which faith has believed
to be truly promised by God.

John Calvin

Hope must be in the future tense.
Faith, to be faith, must always be
in the present tense.

Catherine Marshall

When you accept the fact that sometimes
seasons are dry and times are hard and
that God is in control of both, you will
discover a sense of divine refuge because
the hope then is in God and
not in yourself.

Charles Swindoll

Praise be to the God and Father
of our Lord Jesus Christ! In his
great mercy he has given us
new birth into a living hope
through the resurrection of
Jesus Christ from the dead.

1 Peter 1:3 NIV

Teach us to set our hopes on heaven,
to hold firmly to the promise of eternal
life, so that we can withstand the struggles
and storms of this world.

Max Lucado

Oh, remember this: There is never a time
when we may not hope in God. Whatever
our necessities, however great our
difficulties, and though to all appearance,
help is impossible, yet our business is
to hope in God, and it will be found
that it is not in vain.

George Mueller

This life of faith, then, consists in just
  this—being a child in the Father's house.
  Let the ways of childish confidence and
  freedom from care, which so please you
and win your heart when you observe your
own little ones, teach you what you should
    be in your attitude toward God.
Hannah Whitall Smith

Never yield to gloomy anticipation.
  Place your hope and confidence in God.
      He has no record of failure.
Mrs. Charles E. Cowman

The essence of optimism is that it takes no account of the present, but it is a source of inspiration, of vitality, and of hope. Where others have resigned, it enables a man to hold his head high, to claim the future for himself, and not abandon it to his enemy.

Dietrich Bonhoeffer

Keep your feet on the ground,
but let your heart soar as high
as it will. Refuse to be average
or to surrender to the chill of
your spiritual environment.

A. W. Tozer

Troubles we bear trustfully can bring us
a fresh vision of God and a new outlook
on life, an outlook of peace and hope.
Billy Graham

The Lord Himself has laid the foundation
of His people's hopes. We must determine
if our hopes are built on this foundation.
C. H. Spurgeon

Love is the seed of all hope.
It is the enticement to trust,
to risk, to try, and to go on.
Gloria Gaither

Easter comes each year
to remind us of a truth that
is eternal and universal. The
empty tomb of Easter morning
says to you and me, "Of course
you'll encounter trouble. But
behold a God of power who
can take any evil and turn it
into a door of hope."

Catherine Marshall

Happy is he . . . whose hope
is in the LORD his God.

Psalm 146:5 KJV

Forgiveness

Judge not, and ye shall not be
judged: condemn not, and
ye shall not be condemned:
forgive, and ye shall
be forgiven.

Luke 6:37 KJV

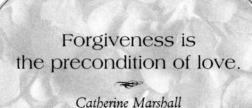

Forgiveness is
the precondition of love.

Catherine Marshall

How often must we forgive family members and friends? More times than we can count. Our children are precious but imperfect; so are our spouses and our friends. We must, on occasion, forgive those who have injured us; to do otherwise is to disobey God.

Are you easily frustrated by the inevitable inconveniences and disappointments of life? If so, perhaps you need a refresher course in the art of forgiveness.

If there exists even one person, alive or dead, whom you have not forgiven (and that includes yourself), follow God's commandment and His will for your life: forgive. Bitterness, anger, and regret are not part of God's plan for your life. Forgiveness is.

Be ye therefore merciful,
as your Father also is merciful.
Luke 6:36 KJV

Are you aware of
the joy-stealing effect
an unforgiving spirit is having
on your life?

❧

Charles Swindoll

Why do you look at the speck of sawdust in your brother's eye and pay no attention to the plank in your own eye? How can you say to your brother, "Let me take the speck out of your eye," when all the time there is a plank in your own eye? You hypocrite, first take the plank out of your own eye, and then you will see clearly to remove the speck from your brother's eye.

Matthew 7:3-5 NIV

Forgiveness is God's command.

Martin Luther

Forgiveness is the key that unlocks
the door of resentment and the handcuffs
of hate. It is a power that breaks
the chains of bitterness and
the shackles of selfishness.

Corrie ten Boom

Our relationships with other people are
of primary importance to God.
Because God is love, He cannot tolerate
any unforgiveness or hardness
in us toward any individual.

Catherine Marshall

Forgiveness

If you are in Christ, when He sees you,
   your sins are covered—He doesn't see
   them. He sees you better than you see
   yourself. And that is a glorious fact
   of your life.

Max Lucado

I believe that forgiveness can become
   a continuing cycle: because God forgives
   us, we're to forgive others; because we
   forgive others, God forgives us. Scripture
   presents both parts of the cycle.

Shirley Dobson

He who cannot forgive others
breaks the bridge over which
he himself must pass.

Corrie ten Boom

Jesus had a forgiving and understanding
heart. If He lives within us, mercy will
temper our relationships
with our fellow men.

Billy Graham

To be a Christian means to forgive
the inexcusable, because God has
forgiven the inexcusable in you.

C. S. Lewis

Give me such love for God and men
as will blot out all hatred and bitterness.

Dietrich Bonhoeffer

Our Savior kneels down and gazes upon the darkest acts of our lives. But rather than recoil in horror, He reaches out in kindness and says, "I can clean that if you want." And, from the basin of His grace, He scoops a palm full of mercy and washes our sin.

Max Lucado

Praise and
Thanksgiving

Rejoice evermore.
Pray without ceasing. In every
thing give thanks: for this
is the will of God in Christ Jesus
concerning you.
1 Thessalonians 5:16-18 KJV

How changed our lives would be if we could only fly through the days on wings of surrender, praise, and trust!

Hannah Whitall Smith

Too many of us, even well-intentioned believers, tend to "compartmentalize" our waking hours into a few familiar categories: work, rest, play, family time, and worship. As creatures of habit, we may find ourselves praising God only at particular times of the day or the week. But praise for our Creator should never be reserved for mealtimes or bedtimes or church. Instead, we should praise God all day, every day, to the greatest extent we can, with thanksgiving in our hearts, and with a song on our lips.

Today, as you hug your child or kiss your spouse, or as you gaze upon a passing cloud or marvel at a glorious sunset, think of what God has done for you and for yours. And, every time you notice a gift from the Giver of all things good, praise Him. His works are marvelous, His gifts are beyond understanding, and His love endures forever.

Surely the righteous shall give thanks unto thy name: the upright shall dwell in thy presence.
Psalm 140:13 KJV

We ought to give thanks for all fortune:
if it is good, because it is good, if bad,
because it works in us patience, humility,
and the contempt of this world, along with
the hope of our eternal country.

C. S. Lewis

God has promised that if we harvest well
with the tools of thanksgiving, there will
be seeds for planting in the spring.

Gloria Gaither

God is in control, and therefore in
everything I can give thanks, not because
of the situation, but because of the One
who directs and rules over it.

Kay Arthur

He upholds the whole creation,
founded the earth, and still
sustains it by the word of His
power. What cannot He do
in the affairs of families and
kingdoms, far beyond our
conception and expectation,
He who hangs the earth
upon nothing?

❧

Matthew Henry

Gratitude changes the pangs
        of memory into a tranquil joy.
                            Dietrich Bonhoeffer

The act of thanksgiving is a demonstration
        of the fact that you are going
            to trust and believe God.
                            Kay Arthur

Let's thank God for allowing us
    to experience troubles that drive
        us closer to Him.

Shirley Dobson

When there is peace in the heart,
    there will be praise on the lips.

Warren Wiersbe

Praise—lifting up our heart and hands,
    exulting with our voices, singing
        His praises—is the occupation of
    those who dwell in the kingdom.

Max Lucado

Let the godly sing with joy
to the LORD, for it is fitting
to praise him.

❧

Psalm 33:1 NLT

You are my God, and I will give you
thanks; you are my God, and I will exalt
you. Give thanks to the LORD, for he is
good; his love endures forever.
Psalm 118:28-29 NIV

Most of the verses written about praise
in God's Word were voiced by people
faced with crushing heartaches, injustice,
treachery, slander, and scores
of other difficult situations.
Joni Eareckson Tada

To praise God is to please God.
Jim Gallery

I will praise the name of God
with a song, and will magnify
him with thanksgiving.

Psalm 69:30 KJV

God's Abundance

I am come that they might have
life, and that they might have it
more abundantly.

John 10:10 KJV

If we were given all we wanted here, our hearts would settle for this world rather than the next.

Elisabeth Elliot

*J*esus promises that we can have abundance through Him. But, every mother knows that some days are so busy and so hurried that abundance seems a distant promise. It is not. Every day, we can claim the spiritual abundance that God promises for our lives . . . and we should.

God's gifts are available to all, but they are not guaranteed; those gifts must be claimed by those who choose to follow Christ. As believers, we are free to accept God's gifts, or not; that choice—and the consequences that result from it—are ours and ours alone. As we go about our daily lives, may we accept God's promise of spiritual abundance, and may we share it with a world in desperate need of the Master's healing touch.

I will lift up mine eyes unto the hills,
from which cometh my help.
Psalm 121:1 KJV

God is the giver,
and we are the receivers.
And His richest gifts are
bestowed not upon those
who do the greatest things,
but upon those who accept
His abundance and His grace.

Hannah Whitall Smith

And God will generously
provide all you need.
Then you will always have
everything you need and plenty
left over to share with others.

2 Corinthians 9:8 NLT

People, places, and things
were never meant to give us
life. God alone is the author
of a fulfilling life.

Gary Smalley & John Trent

Abundant living means
abundant giving.

❧

E. Stanley Jones

It would be wrong to have a "poverty
complex," for to think ourselves paupers
is to deny either the King's riches
or to deny our being His children.

Catherine Marshall

Jesus intended for us to be overwhelmed
by the blessings of regular days. He said
it was the reason He had come: "I am
come that they might have life, and that
they might have it more abundantly."

Gloria Gaither

Visible success has never been
 the proof of Jesus or His followers.
Vance Havner

Get ready for God to show you not
 only His pleasure, but His approval.
Joni Eareckson Tada

You did not choose me, but I chose you
 and appointed you to go and bear fruit—
 fruit that will last. Then the Father will
 give you whatever you ask in my name.
John 15:16 NIV

God loves you and wants you
to experience peace and life—
abundant and eternal.

Billy Graham

When God blesses us, He expects us
to use those blessings to bless
the lives of others.

Jim Gallery

God is more anxious to bestow His
blessings on us than we are
to receive them.

St. Augustine

I will say of the LORD, He is my refuge
and my fortress: my God,
in him I will trust.

Psalm 91:2 KJV

Ask and it will be given to you;
seek and you will find; knock
and the door will be opened
to you. For everyone who asks
receives; he who seeks finds;
and to him who knocks,
the door will be opened.

Matthew 7:7-8 NIV

Courage

For God hath not given us the
spirit of fear; but of power, and
of love, and of a sound mind.

2 Timothy 1:7 KJV

The fear of God is the death of every other fear.

C. H. Spurgeon

Courage

This world can be a dangerous and daunting place, but Christians have every reason to live courageously. After all, the ultimate battle has already been fought and won on the cross at Calvary. But even the most dedicated Christian mom may find her courage tested by the inevitable disappointments and fears that visit the lives of believers and non-believers alike.

The next time you find your courage tested to the limit, remember to take your fears to God. If you call upon Him, you will be comforted. Whatever your challenge, whatever your trouble, God can handle it. And will.

The LORD himself goes before you and will be with you; he will never leave you nor forsake you. Do not be afraid; do not be discouraged.
Deuteronomy 31:8 NIV

If a person fears God, he or she has
no reason to fear anything else. On the
other hand, if a person does not fear God,
then fear becomes a way of life.

Beth Moore

Jesus Christ can make the weakest person
into a divine dreadnought,
fearing nothing.

Oswald Chambers

What is courage?
It is the ability to be strong
in trust, in conviction,
in obedience. To be
courageous is to step out
in faith—to trust and obey,
no matter what.

Kay Arthur

Daniel looked into the face of God
and would not fear the face of a lion.

C. H. Spurgeon

Are you fearful? First, bow your head
and pray for God's strength. Then,
raise your head knowing that, together,
you and God can handle whatever
comes your way.

Jim Gallery

The truth of Christ brings assurance and
so removes the former problem
of fear and uncertainty.

A. W. Tozer

Courage

When once we are assured that God
is good, then there can be
nothing left to fear.
Hannah Whitall Smith

Take courage. We walk in the wilderness
today and in the Promised Land
tomorrow.
D. L. Moody

To fear and not be afraid,
that is the paradox of faith.
A. W. Tozer

Faith is stronger than fear.

John Maxwell

Do not let Satan deceive you into
   being afraid of God's plans for your life.
                                    R. A. Torrey

The Lord is glad to open the gate to every
   knocking soul. It opens very freely; its
   hinges are not rusted; no bolts secure it.
   Have faith and enter at this moment
   through holy courage. If you knock with
   a heavy heart, you shall yet sing with joy
   of spirit. Never be discouraged!
                                    C. H. Spurgeon

The LORD is my light and my
salvation—so why should
I be afraid? The LORD protects
me from danger—so why
should I tremble?

Psalm 27:1 NLT

Celebrating Life

Rejoice in the Lord always.
I will say it again: Rejoice!
Philippians 4:4 HCSB

This is my story,
this is my song, praising my
Savior, all the day long.

Fanny Crosby

*A*re you a mom who celebrates life? Hopefully you are! God has richly blessed you, and He wants you to rejoice in His gifts.

God fills each day to the brim with possibilities, and He challenges each of us to use our gifts for the glory of His kingdom. When we honor the Father and place Him at the center of our lives, every day becomes a cause for celebration.

Today is a non-renewable resource—once it's gone, it's gone forever. Our responsibility—both as mothers and as believers—is to use this day in the service of God's will and in the service of His people. When we do so, we enrich our own lives *and* the lives of those whom we love. And the Father smiles.

Seek the LORD, and ye shall live . . . .
Amos 5:6 KJV

In the great orchestra we call life,
    you have an instrument and a song,
    and you owe it to God to play them
        both sublimely.

Max Lucado

Our God is the sovereign Creator of
    the universe! He loves us as His own
    children and has provided every
    good thing we have; He is worthy
    of our praise every moment.

Shirley Dobson

How delightful a teacher, but gentle
    a provider, how bountiful a giver
    is my Father! Praise, praise to Thee,
        O manifested Most High.

Jim Elliot

Today you will encounter
God's creation. When you see
the beauty around you, let each
detail remind you to lift
your head in praise.

Max Lucado

When we invite Jesus into our lives,
we experience life in the fullest,
most vital sense.

Catherine Marshall

Shout the shout of faith. Nothing can
withstand the triumphant faith that links
itself to omnipotence. For "this is
the victory that overcometh the world."
The secret of all successful living lies
in this shout of faith.

Hannah Whitall Smith

We honor God by asking for great things
when they are part of His promise.
We dishonor Him and cheat ourselves
when we ask for molehills where
He has offered mountains.

Vance Havner

The value of a life can only be estimated
by its relationship to God.

Oswald Chambers

We can be victorious, but only
if we walk with God.

Beth Moore

The responsible person seeks
to make his or her whole life
a response to the question
and call of God.

Dietrich Bonhoeffer

Preoccupy my thoughts with
your praise beginning today.

Joni Eareckson Tada

I will bless them and the places surrounding my hill. I will send down showers in season; there will be showers of blessings.

❧

Ezekiel 34:26 NIV

Faith

But Jesus turned him about,
and when he saw her, he said,
Daughter, be of good comfort;
thy faith hath made thee whole.
And the woman was made
whole from that hour.

Matthew 9:22 KJV

The beginning of anxiety
is the end of faith, and
the beginning of true faith
is the end of anxiety.

George Mueller

*A*re you a mother whose faith is evident for all to see? Do you trust God's promises without reservation, *or* do you question His promises without hesitation?

Every life—including yours—is a series of successes and failures, celebrations and disappointments, joys and sorrows. Every step of the way, through every triumph and tragedy, God will stand by your side and strengthen you . . . if you have faith in Him.

Jesus taught His disciples that if they had faith, they could move mountains. You can, too, and so can your family. But you must have faith. So today and every day, trust your Heavenly Father, praise the sacrifice of His Son . . . and then let the mountain-moving begin.

If you do not stand firm in your faith,
you will not stand at all.
Isaiah 7:9 NIV

Love is an attribute of God.
     To love others is evidence
        of a genuine faith.

Kay Arthur

The whole being of any Christian is Faith
   and Love. Faith brings the man to God;
        love brings Him to men.

Martin Luther

The Christian life has two different
       dimensions: faith toward God
           and love toward men.
       You cannot separate the two.

Warren Wiersbe

Faith is to believe what you do not yet see; the reward for this faith is to see what you believe.

St. Augustine

When you realize that your circumstances,
no matter how overwhelming or pressing,
are ruled by a King who seeks your highest
good, you can truly "consider it all joy . . .
when you encounter various trials,
knowing that the testing of your faith
produces endurance . . . that you may be
perfect and complete, lacking in nothing"
(James 1:2-4).

Charles Swindoll

Just as our faith strengthens our prayer
life, so do our prayers deepen our faith.
Let us pray often, starting today,
for a deeper, more powerful faith.

Shirley Dobson

God doesn't always change
the circumstances, but He can change
us to meet the circumstances.
That's what it means to live by faith.

Warren Wiersbe

True faith does not so much attempt to
manipulate God to do our will
as it does to position us to do His will.

Philip Yancey

Where there are no good works, there is
no faith. If works and love do not blossom
forth, it is not genuine faith, the Gospel
has not yet gained a foothold, and
Christ is not yet rightly known.

Martin Luther

Do something that
demonstrates faith, for faith
with no effort is no faith at all.

Max Lucado

Faith means believing in advance
what will only make sense in reverse.
Philip Yancey

Faith will not always get for us what
we want, but it will get what God
wants us to have.
Vance Havner

Faith never knows where it is being led,
but it loves the One who is leading.
Oswald Chambers

Therefore, being always of
good courage . . . we walk
by faith, not by sight.

2 Corinthians 5:6-7 NASB

Thanks, Mom!

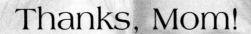

Strength and dignity are her
clothing, and she smiles at the
future. She opens her mouth
in wisdom, and the teaching
of kindness is on her tongue.
She looks well to the ways
of her household.

Proverbs 31:25-27 NASB

Charm is deceptive,
and beauty is fleeting;
but a woman who fears
the LORD is to be praised.
Give her the reward
she has earned . . . .

Proverbs 31:30-31 NIV

Thanks, Mom!

We conclude with a message of thanks
to marvelous mothers everywhere:

Dear Mom,

Thanks for the love, the care, the work, the discipline, the wisdom, the support, and the faith. Thanks for being a concerned parent and a worthy example. Thanks for giving life and for teaching it. Thanks for being patient with me, even when you were tired or frustrated—or both. Thanks for changing diapers and wiping away tears. And thanks for being a godly woman, one worthy of our admiration and our love.

You deserve a smile today, Mom, but you deserve so much more. You deserve our family's undying gratitude. And, you deserve God's love, His grace, and His peace. May you enjoy God's blessings always, and may you never forget how much we love you.

Signed,

Your Loving Family

For surely, O Lord, you bless
the righteous; you surround
them with your favor as
with a shield.

≈

Psalm 5:12 NIV

What is God looking for? He is looking
for men and women whose hearts
are completely His.

Charles Swindoll

Blessed are they who maintain justice,
who constantly do what is right.

Psalm 106:3 NIV

For the wages of sin is death, but
the gift of God is eternal life in
Christ Jesus our Lord.

Romans 6:23 NIV

But the love of the LORD
remains forever with those who
fear him. His salvation extends
to the children's children of
those who are faithful to his
covenant, of those who obey
his commandments!

❧

Psalm 103:17-18 NLT